Language in Motion

Wiggle, Gallop, and Leap with Words

WRITTEN BY
Betsy Franco & Denise Dauler

EDITOR
Carla Hamaguchi

ILLUSTRATOR
Ann Iosa

COVER ILLUSTRATOR
Rick Grayson

DESIGNER
Moonhee Pak

COVER DESIGNER
Barbara Peterson

ART DIRECTOR
Tom Cochrane

PROJECT DIRECTOR
Carolea Williams

© 2000 Creative Teaching Press, Inc., Huntington Beach, CA 92649
Reproduction of activities in any manner for use in the classroom and not for commercial sale is permissible.
Reproduction of these materials for an entire school or for a school system is strictly prohibited.

Table of Contents

Introduction 3

Getting Started 4

Concepts about Print 5
    A-Hunting We Will Go
    Alphabet Animal Exercises
    Alphabet Path
    Big and Little Letter Match
    Letter Circus
    Letter Magicians
    Sentence Scramble
    Name Hunt
    Slither like a Snake
    Walking It Out

Phonemic Awareness 27
    Bagging It Relay
    Cat, Cat, Bat
    Rime Buses
    Rhyme Hop-a-Long
    Rolling Rimes
    Rime Tunnels
    Blending Endings Hopscotch
    Wiggle to the Sound
    Word Cheers
    You Put Your /H/ Hand In
    Jumping Jamboree
    Word Hunt

Decoding and Word Recognition 54
    Beginning Consonant Relay
    Acting out Vowel Poems
    Compound Word Partners
    Let's Make a Word!
    Web-Go-Round
    Matt's Moving like a Monkey
    Sight Word Wheel
    Word Taxis
    Word Toss
    Magic "E" Relay

Vocabulary and Concept Development .. 78
    Musical Word Chairs
    People Word Wall
    Teacher, May I?
    Directional Poetry
    Opposites Attract
    Jungle Hike
    Charades

Language Skills Inventory 94

Music & Literature Links 95

Gross Motor Skills Index 96

Introduction

Why not give young children the chance to move, use their bodies, and play physical games—all while learning early-language concepts? It's a perfect combination for young children whose natural tendency is to move around. The activities in *Language in Motion* have a magical effect on children because they combine the physical with the cognitive. Children participate enthusiastically and take more ownership of their learning because their own bodies are involved.

On the cognitive level, *Language in Motion* activities encourage children to explore letter recognition; letter writing; beginning, middle, and ending sounds; syllables; onsets and rimes; short and long vowels; rhyming words; action, color, shape, and number words; position words; high-frequency words; left-to-right orientation; and sentence building. On the physical level, children run, jump, slide, crawl, gallop, leap, wiggle, hop, tiptoe, and throw as they practice a variety of gross motor skills and gain a sense of their own personal space. Because children practice physical skills at their own developmental level, they increase their confidence in their bodies *and* their language skills.

With activities for small- and whole-group instruction, *Language in Motion* provides a variety of opportunities to assess and observe individuals because the lessons are designed to allow for individual differences. Children's actions, expressions, and responses will tell you worlds about their developmental levels, both physically and cognitively.

Each fun "language-and-movement" activity requires everyday materials and is quick and simple to set up. Detailed instructions and a variety of reproducibles keep teacher preparation time to a minimum. Use the language skills inventory and the gross motor skills index to decide which activities focus on the developmental needs of your students. Use the variation ideas to adapt each activity to best meet the unique needs and skills of your class. Incorporate the recommended music and literature links to extend the learning and fun. Just think how exciting language can be when it's connected to movement!

Getting Started

The activities in *Language in Motion* are divided into sections based on the language concept each activity introduces. However, many of the activities cover more than one language concept. Each activity page lists all the language concepts featured in that lesson. Each activity page includes four sections:

Get Ready lists the necessary materials.
Get Set describes the teacher preparation.
Go! outlines the step-by-step directions.
Variations are ideas for making the activity easier or more difficult. (Materials and language concepts related to the variations are not listed on the activity page.)

Teacher Preparation

Minimal teacher preparation is required for most of the activities. Some activities require children to wear letter-card or word-card necklaces. The necklaces are made in the same way; the only difference is in the reproducible cards required. Use the following directions to make these student necklaces:

1. Copy the reproducible cards as noted in the Get Set section.

2. Cut apart the cards, and laminate them for durability.

3. Hole-punch the top corners of each card. Tie one end of a piece of yarn or string to each hole.

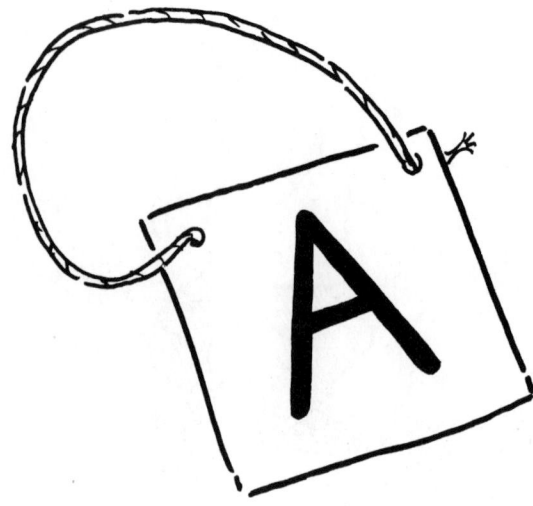

Assessment & Observation

The first page of each main section features a list of questions to ask yourself when children are doing the language-and-movement activities. These questions address the main language goals of the activities in that section. Use the Language Skills Inventory (page 94) to chart each child's progress. Carry the inventory on a clipboard. Mark a plus for mastery, a check for satisfactory progress, and a minus for lack of progress. Use this inventory to see at a glance which skills each child needs to develop.

Music & Literature Links

Because music lends itself to movement, this book includes a list of songs in addition to recommended books (see page 95). Some of the music suggestions are popular children's songs that have been recorded by many different artists. Use the recommended books to reinforce language concepts such as alphabetical order, rhyming words, and alliteration.

Gross Motor Skills Index

Each activity involves at least one type of gross motor skill. Use the index on page 96 to quickly find which activities allow children to develop their hand-eye coordination or their locomotor, nonlocomotor, or balance skills.

4 Getting Started

Concepts about Print

Concepts about print refer to the understanding of what print represents and how it works. The activities in this section will help children with letter recognition and formation, matching uppercase and lowercase letters, print directionality, and formation of words and sentences.

ASSESSMENT & OBSERVATION QUESTIONS

- Can children follow words from left to right? top to bottom?

- Do children recognize and name all uppercase letters? lowercase letters?

- Can children distinguish letters from words?

- Do children recognize that sentences are made up of separate words?

- Can children match spoken words to printed words?

A-Hunting We Will Go

- "Hunting Chant" (page 7)
- letter cards (pages 8–13)
- scissors

LANGUAGE CONCEPTS

letter recognition, rhyming words

1. Have children sit together in a group, and tell them that you have hidden letter cards around the room. Invite each child to find one card.

2. Have children tiptoe back to the group and sit down after they find a card. Encourage children to sit in one or two rows so that they can easily come forward to follow instructions.

3. Recite "Hunting Chant." Invite children to follow the directions based on their letter. For example, when you say *If you found an A, B, C, D, or E, then jump your letter to me*, invite children with the matching letter cards to jump towards you.

4. Collect the letter cards, hide them again, and repeat the activity.

Make enough copies of the letter cards for a–z or A–Z to give one to each child. Cut apart the cards, and scatter them around the classroom.

If you found an A, B, C, D, or E, then jump your letter to me.

VARIATION

- Replace the letters in the chant with number or rhyming words (e.g., *If you found an eight, nine, or ten, skip up and back again* or *If you found a bee, key, or sea, jump your word to me*).

6 *Concepts about Print*

Hunting Chant

A-hunting we will go.
A-hunting we will go.
If you found an A, B, C, D, or E,
Then jump your letter to me.

If you found an F, G, H, I, or J,
Then hippity-hop this way.

If you found a K, L, M, or N,
Skip up and back again.

If you found an O, P, Q, or R,
Walk backward just this far.

If you found an S, T, U, or V,
Then skip right up to me.

If you found a W, X, Y, or Z,
Give a big high-five to me!

Uppercase Letter Cards

A	B	C
D	E	F
G	H	I

Uppercase Letter Cards

J	K	L
M	N	O
P	Q	R

Uppercase Letter Cards

S	T	U
V	W	X
Y	Z	

Lowercase Letter Cards

a	b	c
d	e	f
g	h	i

Lowercase Letter Cards

j	k	l
m	n	o
p	q	r

Concepts about Print

Lowercase Letter Cards

s	t	u
v	w	x
y	z	

Alphabet Animal Exercises

GET READY

- no materials required

LANGUAGE CONCEPT

alphabetical order

GET SET

no preparation required

GO!

1. Have children stand an arm's length apart from each other.

2. Invite children to stretch and exercise as they recite the following chants and perform the movements:

- Giraffe Neck Stretch

We're tall giraffes.
We stretch our necks—
A, B, C, D. (Rotate neck clockwise.)
We stretch our necks
The other way—
E, F, Geeeee! (Rotate neck counterclockwise.)

- Bear Shoulder Roll

We roll our shoulders forward—
H, I, J. (Roll shoulders forward.)
We roll our shoulders back—
K, L, M. (Roll shoulders backward.)
That's how we stretch and loosen them!

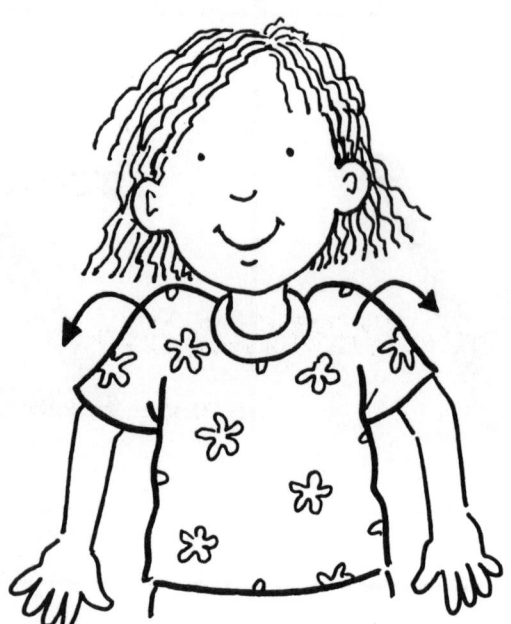

- no materials required

- no preparation required

- Kangaroo Jumping Jacks
  We're jumpy, jumpy kangaroos—
  N, O, P, Q.   (Do 4 jumping jacks.)
  We jump and jump. That's what we do—
  R, S, T, U!   (Do 4 jumping jacks.)

- Monkey Movements
  V   (Touch head.)
  W   (Touch waist.)
  X   (Touch toes.)
  Y   (Touch waist.)
  Z   (Touch head.)
  We're silly monkeys, don't you see?

VARIATION

- Vary the animals used in each chant (e.g., frog jumping jacks).

Concepts about Print **15**

Alphabet Path

- letter cards (pages 8–13)
- scissors
- tape or chalk

LANGUAGE CONCEPT

letter recognition

1. Invite children to walk along the alphabet path and recite each letter as they pass it.

2. Have children vary the locomotor movement. For example, instead of walking, have them jump, hop, or tiptoe.

Copy and cut apart a set of letter cards for a–z or A–Z. Tape the cards in alphabetical order onto the floor to create a path, or use chalk to draw boxes and letters to form a path on the playground.

VARIATIONS

- Write the letters in a pattern, such as *S, B, C, B, V, B, M, B*, on the path. Have children walk on all the *B*'s.

- For older children, write words such as *tap, top, bed, tip, dog, tin,* and *ten* on the path. Encourage children to walk on all the words that start with *t.* Have children say each word before they step on it.

16 Concepts about Print

Big and Little Letter Match

LANGUAGE CONCEPT

matching uppercase and lowercase letters

GET READY

- letter cards (pages 8–13)
- paper (assorted colors)
- scissors
- chalk

GET SET

Copy one set of uppercase letter cards on white paper and one set of lowercase letter cards on colored paper. Cut apart the cards. Use chalk to draw a circle large enough for children to walk around. Place the lowercase letter cards in random order inside the circle, facing outward, so children can read them as they are walking around the circle.

GO!

1. Give each child an uppercase letter card.

2. Invite children to walk around the circle and look for the lowercase version of their letter as they chant the following verse:
   I'm looking for my letter.
   Where can it be?
   It's inside the circle,
   Waiting for me!

3. Say *Freeze*, and ask children to tiptoe to their matching letter card. Encourage them to pick it up and return to the outside of the circle.

4. Invite each child to hold his or her letter cards so the others can see them and say the letter name.

5. Collect the letter cards, place the lowercase letter cards back inside the circle, give each child a new uppercase letter card, and repeat the activity.

VARIATION

- For younger children, use only two sets of uppercase letter cards. Or, use a limited number of letters rather than the whole alphabet.

Concepts about Print **17**

Letter Circus

- letter cards (pages 8–13)
- scissors

Copy and cut apart a set of letter cards (either upper- or lowercase).

LANGUAGE CONCEPT

letter recognition and formation

1 Divide the class into groups of four.

2 Tell children they will form the letters one by one for the "Letter Circus."

3 Write the letter *A* on the chalkboard. Invite four children to lie down to make an *A* with their bodies.

4 Give four to six letter cards to each group, and encourage children to use their bodies to make the letters on their cards.

5 Have the whole class sit, and begin the Letter Circus. Invite groups to take turns making their letters as you announce them. For example, say *In this ring, we have the letter* C, and have the group with the *C* card make the letter *C* for the rest of the class.

VARIATIONS

- For younger children, use just a few letters or a group of letters on which the class has been working.
- Have older children form three letters at a time to create a word (e.g., *c, a, t*).

Concepts about Print

Letter Magicians

- tape
- crepe or tissue paper
- sticks or rulers

LANGUAGE CONCEPT

letter recognition and formation

1. Have children stand an arm's length apart from each other. Give each child a magic wand.

2. Write a letter on the chalkboard. Stand with your back to the class, and use your magic wand to write the letter in the air.

3. Describe the movements as you make them. For example, say *down, down, across* when you make *A*.

4. Have children say the name of the letter, and encourage them to follow your movements to make it.

5. Repeat the activity with the remaining letters of the alphabet.

Tape crepe or tissue paper to sticks or rulers to make one "magic wand" for each child and one for yourself.

VARIATIONS

- Have older children create the letters without your model.
- Have younger children make only the letters on which the class has been working.

Concepts about Print

Sentence Scramble

LANGUAGE CONCEPTS

building sentences, left-to-right directionality, sight words

- Sentence Word Cards (pages 21–23)
- index cards

Use the sentence word cards to make word necklaces (see page 4). You will have three sets of necklaces (e.g., *dogs, like, to, chase,* and *cats* are one set). Have blank index cards available for groups who want to add a word to their sentence.

1. Divide the class into groups of at least seven children. Give each group a set of sentence word cards. Choose two children to be the "sentence-makers" for each group, and ask the other children in the group to put on a word necklace. Encourage children to read the word on their necklace as they put it on.

2. Encourage the sentence-makers to arrange the children in their group so that the words on their necklaces form sentences.

3. Challenge children to make more than one sentence with their group of words (e.g., *dogs like to chase cats* can be changed to *cats like dogs* or *dogs chase cats*).

4. Have groups trade sets of sentence word cards, and designate different children to be sentence-makers. Have children repeat the activity.

VARIATION

- Have each group write their sentence on a piece of paper. Encourage groups to draw a picture that corresponds with their sentence. Put all their pages together to make a class book.

Sentence Word Cards

dogs	chase
like	
to	cats

Sentence Word Cards

Bill	eats	pizza

and	cake

Sentence Word Cards

Mary

likes

Dad and Mom

Name Hunt

- name tags
- index cards

Write each child's name on a nametag and an index card. Scatter the cards around the classroom (e.g., on tables, chairs, or the floor).

LANGUAGE CONCEPT

letter recognition and sounds

1. Have children sit together in a group, and give each child a name tag to wear.
2. Tell children to gallop around the room and pick up a classmate's name card.
3. Invite children to use baby steps to deliver the name card to its owner.
4. When all children are seated, invite them to take turns jumping up, displaying their name tag, and saying their name.

VARIATION

- For older children, eliminate the set of name tags that children are wearing so they have to sound out the letters to figure out whose name card they have.

24 Concepts about Print

Slither like a Snake

LANGUAGE CONCEPTS

letter recognition and formation, letter sounds

- no materials required

1. Write a letter on the chalkboard, and say the letter name as you exaggerate its sound (e.g., *ssss* for the letter *S*).

2. Invite children to "be" the letter. Suggest a creative movement associated with that letter (e.g., S *ssslithers like a sssnake*).
   Here are suggestions for each letter of the alphabet that emphasize the name, sound, and shape of the letter:

no preparation required

A holds **a**n **a**rmful of **a**pples.
B is a **b**us **b**umping along.
C **c**urls up like a **c**at.
D is **d**iving like a **d**olphin.
E is an **e**lephant with **e**ars that flap.
F has **f**ingers reaching like **f**luttering **f**lags.
G **g**ives food at a **g**ood restaurant.
H is two people **h**olding **h**ands.
I **i**s as straight as an **i**cicle.
J **j**umps for **j**oy.
K **k**icks a ball.
L **l**ooks **l**ike an elbow.
M is a **m**ountain that is hard to **m**ove.

N is a **n**oodle, **n**eatly going up and down.
O is like the hole **o**n a d**o**nut.
P is a **p**enguin **p**uffing out its chest.
Q is kicking out **q**uickly.
R is a **r**eindeer **r**unning in the woods.
S **s**lithers like a **s**nake.
T is a **t**abletop set for **t**ea.
U reaches **u**p to hold an **u**mbrella.
V is love, looking for a hug.
W is **w**avy like the **w**ater in the ocean.
X stretches arms and legs e**x**tra big.
Y **y**awns and stretches when it gets up.
Z **z**igzags like a butterfly in the garden.

VARIATION

- Challenge children to write their own sentences or create a movement for each letter.

Concepts about Print 25

Walking It Out

- chalk or tape

LANGUAGE CONCEPT

letter recognition and formation

1. Stand beside a letter, and have children line up behind you. Tell children that you are the leader, and invite them to follow you as you walk on the letter.

2. As you lead the class over the letter, describe the motion you are making (e.g., say *Down and across for the letter* L).

3. Follow the same procedure for the next letter. Choose a different motion for children to do (e.g., hop).

Use chalk to write large letters on the playground, or use tape to make letters on an indoor floor. For younger children, make two or three letters. Add more letters for older children.

VARIATION

- Write out words on the ground, and have older children hop or crawl on the words.

26 Concepts about Print

Phonemic Awareness

Phonemic awareness is the knowledge of how language works. It is the ability to hear the sounds (phonemes) that make up words, to see relationships between sounds, and to alter or rearrange sounds to create new words. The following activities provide children with opportunities to identify rhyming words; hear long and short vowels; blend sounds to make words; and identify beginning, middle, and ending sounds.

ASSESSMENT & OBSERVATION QUESTIONS

- Can children identify and produce rhyming words?

- Can children count the number of syllables in a word?

- Can children distinguish the beginning sound in a single syllable word? ending sound? middle sound?

- Can children distinguish between long and short vowels?

- Can children blend sounds orally to make a word?

- Can children change or delete a sound to change words?

Bagging It Relay

- Picture Cards (pages 29–32)
- scissors
- paper lunch sacks

Copy and cut apart the picture cards. Write each of the following letters on a lunch sack: *b, d, g, p, t, l, n, s, m,* and *r*. Place the bags in a line to form a finish line for the relay.

LANGUAGE CONCEPT

ending consonant sounds

1. Divide the class into two relay teams. Have children line up single file, about 20' (6 m) from the finish line. Explain to children that this is a noncompetitive relay. The goal is to complete the task correctly, not to finish it in a hurry.

2. Give each child a picture card.

3. Have the first two children say what picture is on their card. Encourage them to stress the ending sound when saying the word. Have the children run down and place their card in the bag with the matching ending sound. For example, a child with a picture of a crib, says *crib /b/* and puts the card in the bag with a *b* on it.

4. Continue with the next child in each line. Repeat the activity until each child has had a turn.

5. When all the picture cards have been bagged, have everyone sit in a circle and go through each bag together as a class. Encourage children to pronounce the words with an emphasis on the ending consonants.

VARIATION

- Have children practice ending sounds with consonant blends and digraphs. (Use the picture cards on pages 33–34.) Write one of the following blends on each bag: *nk, th, sh, ch, ng,* and *ck*.

28 Phonemic Awareness

Picture Cards

Picture Cards

Picture Cards

Phonemic Awareness

Picture Cards

Picture Cards—Ending Digraphs

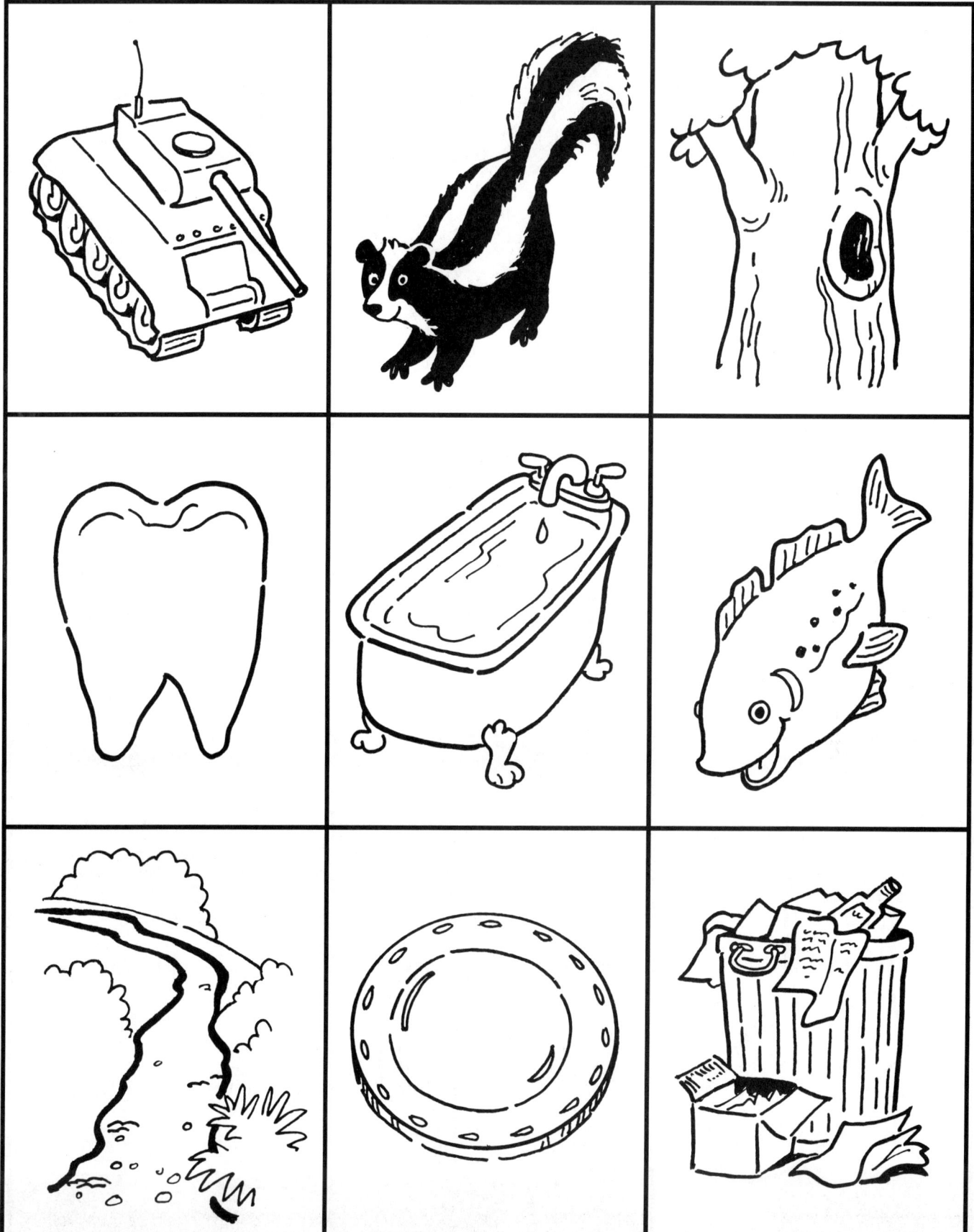

Picture Cards—Ending Digraphs

Cat, Cat, Bat

● no materials required

LANGUAGE CONCEPTS

rhyming words, short and long vowels

1 Have children sit in a large circle on the floor.

2 Choose one child to be the "tapper." Invite the tapper to walk around the circle, tap the head of each child, and say the word *cat*.

3 After the tapper taps a few children's heads, invite him or her to tap a child's head and say a word that rhymes with cat (e.g., *bat*).

4 Prompt the last child who was tapped to get up and chase the tapper around the outside of the circle. Encourage the tapper to run to the empty place in the circle before the tagger tags him or her.

5 Invite the tagged child to become the tapper, and repeat the activity.

no preparation required

VARIATION

● Have children help you create new refrains (e.g., *pig, pig, dig* or *bee, bee, flea*).

Phonemic Awareness

Rime Buses

- Rime Word List (page 37)
- index cards

LANGUAGE CONCEPTS

onsets and rimes, rhyming words, short and long vowel sounds

Choose four rimes from the Rime Word List, and write each rime on a separate index card. Write several rhyming words for each rime on separate index cards (e.g., *cat, bat, mat, sat, hat,* and *flat* for the rime *-at*). Use the rhyming word cards to make word necklaces (see page 4).

1. Choose four children to act as bus drivers, and give each one a rime card to hold. Tell the other children they will be "passengers," and give each one a word necklace.

2. Encourage children to stand at a "bus stop," or assign them to one. Make sure that there are children with different rime words at each bus stop.

3. Have each bus driver walk to a bus stop. Tell children to "board the bus" if the rime on the driver's card is in their word. Tell children who board the bus to place their hands on the shoulders of the person in front of them. Encourage children to sing "The Wheels on the Bus" as the bus moves from stop to stop. Repeat the activity until each bus driver has visited each stop.

4. Have the buses line up beside each other in front of the class. Encourage the driver to say the "bus rime" and the passengers to say their word.

5. Choose new bus drivers. Have children trade necklaces, and repeat the activity.

VARIATIONS

- Have the bus drivers hold a word card, such as *cat*, instead of the rime card.
- When passengers say their word in front of the class, encourage them to say which onset was added to the rime to make their word. For example, a child says /b/ *was added to* -at *to make* bat.

36 *Phonemic Awareness*

Rime Word List

-ag	-ake	-an	-at	-ed
bag	bake	ban	bat	bed
drag	brake	can	cat	fed
flag	cake	fan	flat	led
nag	flake	plan	hat	red
rag	lake	ran	mat	shed
tag	make	tan	pat	sled
wag	rake	van	rat	wed
	shake		sat	
	snake		scat	
	take			

-eep	-eet	-ide	-ine	-ip
beep	beet	bride	dine	chip
deep	feet	glide	fine	clip
jeep	fleet	hide	line	dip
keep	greet	ride	mine	flip
peep	meet	side	nine	hip
seep	street	slide	shine	lip
sheep	sweet	tide	spine	rip
sleep		wide	vine	ship
steep				skip
sweep				tip
				zip

-oke	-one	-op	-ot	-ug
broke	bone	chop	cot	bug
choke	cone	cop	dot	chug
coke	lone	drop	hot	dug
joke	phone	hop	pot	hug
poke	shone	mop	rot	mug
smoke	stone	pop	shot	plug
woke	tone	shop	spot	rug
	zone	stop	trot	slug
		top		snug

Rhyme Hop-a-Long

LANGUAGE CONCEPT

rhyming words

GET READY

- Hop-a-Long Poems (page 39)
- chart paper
- highlighter

GET SET

Write each poem on a separate piece of chart paper. Highlight all the rhyming words in each poem.

GO!

1. Read aloud the first poem as you clap the rhythm of the poem.

2. Reread the poem, and encourage children to read along with you.

3. Encourage children to listen for rhyming words. Have children hop on one leg each time they hear a rhyming word.

4. Repeat the activity with another poem and a different movement (e.g., jump, gallop).

Postman, postman,
Let me [see].
How many letters
Are for [me]?

See! Me!

VARIATIONS

- Change the rhyming words to make new verses.
- Invite children to highlight the rhyming words.

38 *Phonemic Awareness*

Hop-a-Long Poems

My sister went to town

To see what she could see.

But all my sister saw

Was the deep blue sea.

Annie picked some apples.

Peter picked some pears.

Then they sat down

And ate them on the stairs.

Once I had five pennies

That I traded for a nickel.

I went to Silly Sally's store

And bought myself a pickle.

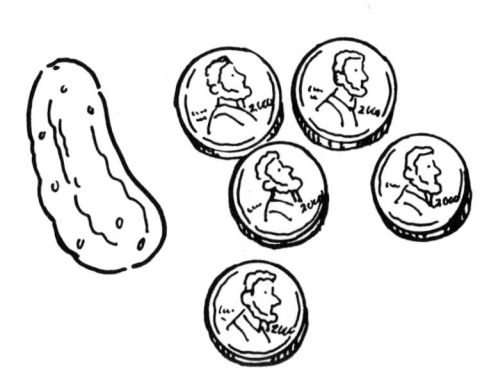

Postman, postman,

Let me see.

How many letters

Are for me?

Rolling Rimes

GET READY

- Onset Cards (page 41)
- Rime Cards (page 42)
- rubber ball

GET SET

Make several copies of the onset cards and the rime cards. Use the cards to make necklaces (see page 4). Half the class will need onset necklaces and the other half will need rime necklaces.

LANGUAGE CONCEPT

blending onsets and rimes

GO!

1. Invite children to sit in two parallel lines facing each other with about 5' (1.5 m) between them.

2. Give each child in one line an onset necklace and each child in the other line a rime necklace.

3. Give a rubber ball to a child in the onset line, and encourage the child to say the sound of his or her onset and roll the ball to someone in the other line.

4. Ask the child who receives the ball to say the sound of his or her rime. Then, encourage both children to blend their two sounds to form a word. For example, the first child says /m/, the second child says /ine/, and together they say *mine*.

5. Have the second child return the ball to someone in the onset line, and repeat the activity.

VARIATION

- Have children wear letter necklaces and pass the ball between the two lines until they form a word. For example, a child wearing a *b*, rolls it to a child wearing an *a*, who rolls it to a child wearing a *g* to form the word *bag*.

40 *Phonemic Awareness*

Onset Cards

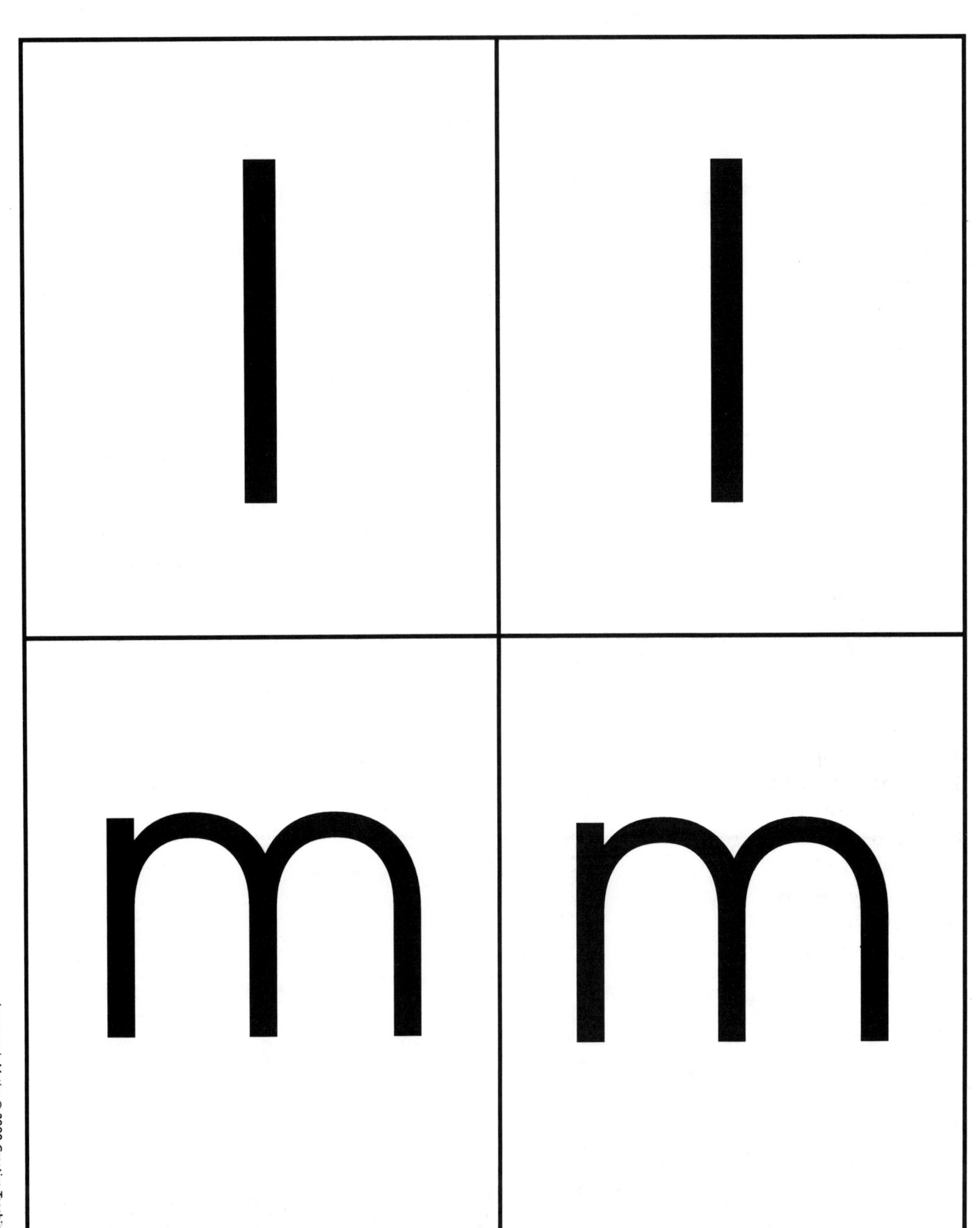

l	l
m	m

Phonemic Awareness

Rime Cards

-ine	-ake
-ean	-ane
-ice	-ime

Rime Tunnels

GET READY

- Rime Tunnel Cards (page 44)
- Onset Cards (page 45)
- scissors
- glue
- poster board

GET SET

Copy and cut apart the rime tunnel cards. Glue each tunnel card to a separate piece of poster board, and fold each piece in half so children can read the cards. Make enough copies of the onset cards to give one to each child, and cut them apart.

LANGUAGE CONCEPTS

blending onsets and rimes, rhyming words

GO!

1. Choose four pairs of children to hold hands and raise their arms overhead to form "tunnels." Arrange pairs of children to create a circular path.

2. Place a rime card by each tunnel. Hold up each rime card, and have the class recite the sounds. Give each of the other children an onset card.

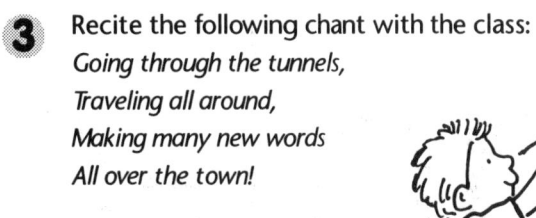

3. Recite the following chant with the class:
   Going through the tunnels,
   Traveling all around,
   Making many new words
   All over the town!

4. Have children stand in a line at one of the tunnels. Ask the first child to say the sound of his or her letter (e.g., /m/) and go through the tunnel. Have the children forming that tunnel say the sound of their rime card (e.g., -ap). Ask children to combine the sounds to make a word (i.e., map).

5. Have children proceed in a circle through all the tunnels. Repeat the activity until each child has gone through all the tunnels.

VARIATION

- Make a new set of cards. Place onset cards at the tunnels, and give children going through the tunnels rime cards.

Phonemic Awareness

Rime Tunnel Cards

-ake

-ug

-ap

-ight

44 Phonemic Awareness

Onset Cards

t	l
t	l
w	r
w	r

Phonemic Awareness

Blending Endings Hopscotch

GET READY

- Sound Cards (page 47)
- chalk

GET SET

Use the sound cards to make a sound necklace for each child (see page 4). Use chalk to draw several hopscotch patterns on the playground (as shown). Write *t*, *n*, or *d* in each hopscotch square.

LANGUAGE CONCEPTS

blending sounds, ending sounds

GO!

1. Divide the class into groups of six, and assign each group to a hopscotch pattern.

2. Give each child in a group a different sound necklace.

3. Have children take turns hopping on the hopscotch pattern. Encourage them to blend the sound on their necklace with the sound in the hopscotch square as they land on it. For example, a child with a *ma* necklace hops on a *t* square and says *mat*.

4. Have children exchange necklaces, and repeat the activity.

VARIATIONS

- Have children wear onset necklaces, and write corresponding rimes in the hopscotch squares.
- Write letters in the hopscotch squares, and have younger children practice letter recognition.

Phonemic Awareness

Sound Cards

ma_	pa_
fa_	be_
bi_	bu_

Phonemic Awareness

Wiggle to the Sound

GET READY

- no materials required

LANGUAGE CONCEPTS

beginning, middle, and ending sounds

GO!

1. Have children stand an arm's length apart from each other. Tell children they will be listening for and acting out the three sounds in each word you say.

2. Say a three-letter word, say each letter sound, and perform a movement for each letter sound. For example, say *rib*, say /r/ and clap your hands, say /i/ and wiggle, and say /b/ and lift your arms in the air. As you say each word, draw out each sound so children hear the beginning, middle, and ending sounds (e.g., *rrrrriiiiiib*).

3. Invite children to perform the movements and say the letter sounds.

4. Repeat the activity using different words and movements.

GET SET

no preparation required

VARIATION

- Have children do actions that form the letter. For example, if you say *Y*, have children stand with their legs together and their arms spread out overhead.

48 Phonemic Awareness

Word Cheers

GET READY

- letter cards (pages 11–13)

GET SET

Use one set of lowercase letter cards to make a letter necklace for each child (see page 4). If you have more than 26 children, make extra vowel necklaces.

LANGUAGE CONCEPTS

beginning, middle, and ending sounds; forming words

GO!

1. Give each child a letter necklace, and have children sit down.

2. Tell children they will be cheerleaders and will come to the front of the room and jump in the air when you say their letter. For example, say *Give me a* C, and ask the child with the *c* card to come forward. Have the class say the letter while that child jumps in the air with his or her hands raised.

3. Continue to call out letters until you have spelled a word (e.g., *Give me a* C. *Give me an* A. *Give me a* P. *What does that spell?*).

4. Have the class repeat those letters as the cheerleaders jump again. Encourage the class to blend the three sounds to make a word (e.g., /c/ /a/ /p/, *cap!*).

5. Substitute one or two letters in the word *cap* to form other words. For example, for the word *map*, have the child with the *m* card join the children with *a* and *p* cards. Repeat the activity using different words.

VARIATION

- Encourage children to think of their own words and cheers.

Phonemic Awareness **49**

You Put Your /H/ Hand In

GET READY

● no materials required

SET

no preparation required

LANGUAGE CONCEPT

initial sounds

GO!

1. Have children stand and form a large circle.

2. Teach children the song "Hootchie Kootchie," and emphasize the initial sounds of words.
   (Sung to the tune of "Hokey Pokey")
   You put your /h/ hand in.
   You put your /h/ hand in.
   You put your /h/ hand in
   And you shake it all about.
   You do the hootchie kootchie
   And you shake yourself around.
   That's what it's all about!

3. Use different verses to emphasize different initial sounds. For example, replace the word *hand* with *foot* so the new verse is *You put your /f/ foot in.*

♪ *You put your /h/ hand in and you shake it all about.* ♪

VARIATION

● Have children think of other body parts and initial sounds to include in the song.

50 Phonemic Awareness

Jumping Jamboree

GET READY

- no materials required

SET

no preparation required

LANGUAGE CONCEPT

syllables

GO!

1. Have children stand at least an arm's length apart from each other.

2. Invite children to do jumping jacks as they chant the following verse:
   *We'll say our names
   And jump to the beat.
   It's time for the
   Jumping-jack jamboree!*

3. Say a child's name. Encourage children to say each syllable in that name as they do jumping jacks. Clap out each syllable as children do their jumping jacks.

4. Repeat the activity with another name. Be sure to use each child's name at least once.

VARIATIONS

- Substitute other movements for jumping jacks, such as twisting waists and moving arms from side to side.
- Have children jump to each child's first and last name.
- Use this exercise for roll call. For example, have children jump to sentences such as *Jim my is here. Ka ra is not here.*

Phonemic Awareness

Word Hunt

GET READY

- Word Hunt Cards (page 53)
- scissors
- yellow crayon or marker

GET SET

Copy and cut apart one set of word cards. Make another set of word cards, and color the first letter of each word yellow. Cut apart the cards, and cut the first letter of each word off to form separate onset and rime cards (e.g., cut *hot* into two pieces, *h* and *ot*).

LANGUAGE CONCEPTS

onsets and rimes, short vowels

GO!

1. Give an onset or rime card to each child.

2. Give children with onset cards a word card that matches the onset on their card. For example, give the word card *met* to the child with the *m* onset card.

3. Invite children to look for a classmate to form the word on their word card. Have a child with an *m* card look for the child with the *-et* card to form *met*.

4. Once children have found their partner, invite pairs to read their onset, rime, and word to the class (e.g., /m/, *-et, met*).

VARIATION

- Encourage children to form words on their own. If some children could not find a correct match, explain that some letters can be added to more than one ending to make a word (e.g., *m* can be added to *-ap, -at, -et,* and *-op*). As a group, rearrange the partners so that everyone has a correct match.

Phonemic Awareness

Word Hunt Cards

cap	tip
met	hot
run	cat
sit	hen
mop	rub

Decoding and Word Recognition

ASSESSMENT & OBSERVATION QUESTIONS

- Can children match all consonant sounds to appropriate letters?

- Can children match all vowel sounds to appropriate letters?

- Can children read high-frequency words?

- Do children understand that as letters of words change, so do the sounds?

- Can children form compound words?

Decoding means learning how to read printed words fluently and automatically. In the beginning stages, this means having children match consonant and vowel sounds to appropriate letters, reading simple one-syllable and high-frequency words, and understanding that as letters of words change, so do the sounds. In this section, children will practice sound matching, making compound words, and reading high-frequency words.

Beginning Consonant Relay

LANGUAGE CONCEPT

initial consonant sounds

GET READY

- letter cards (pages 11–13)
- Picture Cards (pages 56–58)
- scissors
- chalk or tape

GET SET

Copy and cut apart the letter cards. Use the consonant cards to make a set of letter necklaces (see page 4). Copy and cut apart the picture cards. Use chalk or tape to make a starting line, and place the picture cards 15'–20' (5–6 m) away from the line.

GO!

1. Divide the class into two teams, and have teams line up single file behind the starting line.

2. Give each child a letter necklace.

3. Have the first two children in line make the sound of their consonant. Invite those children to skip, hop, or gallop down to retrieve a picture card that matches their letter. Explain to children that this is not a race; the goal is only to find a picture card that matches their letter.

4. Once children have returned, have them repeat the sound of their consonant along with the name of their object. Have the rest of the class repeat the sound and name.

5. Have the two children go to the end of their line, and invite the next two children to repeat the process. Continue the activity until every child has had a turn.

VARIATIONS

- Eliminate the letter necklaces. Tell children the initial sounds, and have them find a picture card that matches the sound.
- Add the vowel letter cards and picture cards to the activity.

Decoding and Word Recognition **55**

Picture Cards

56 Decoding and Word Recognition

Picture Cards

Decoding and Word Recognition 57

Picture Cards

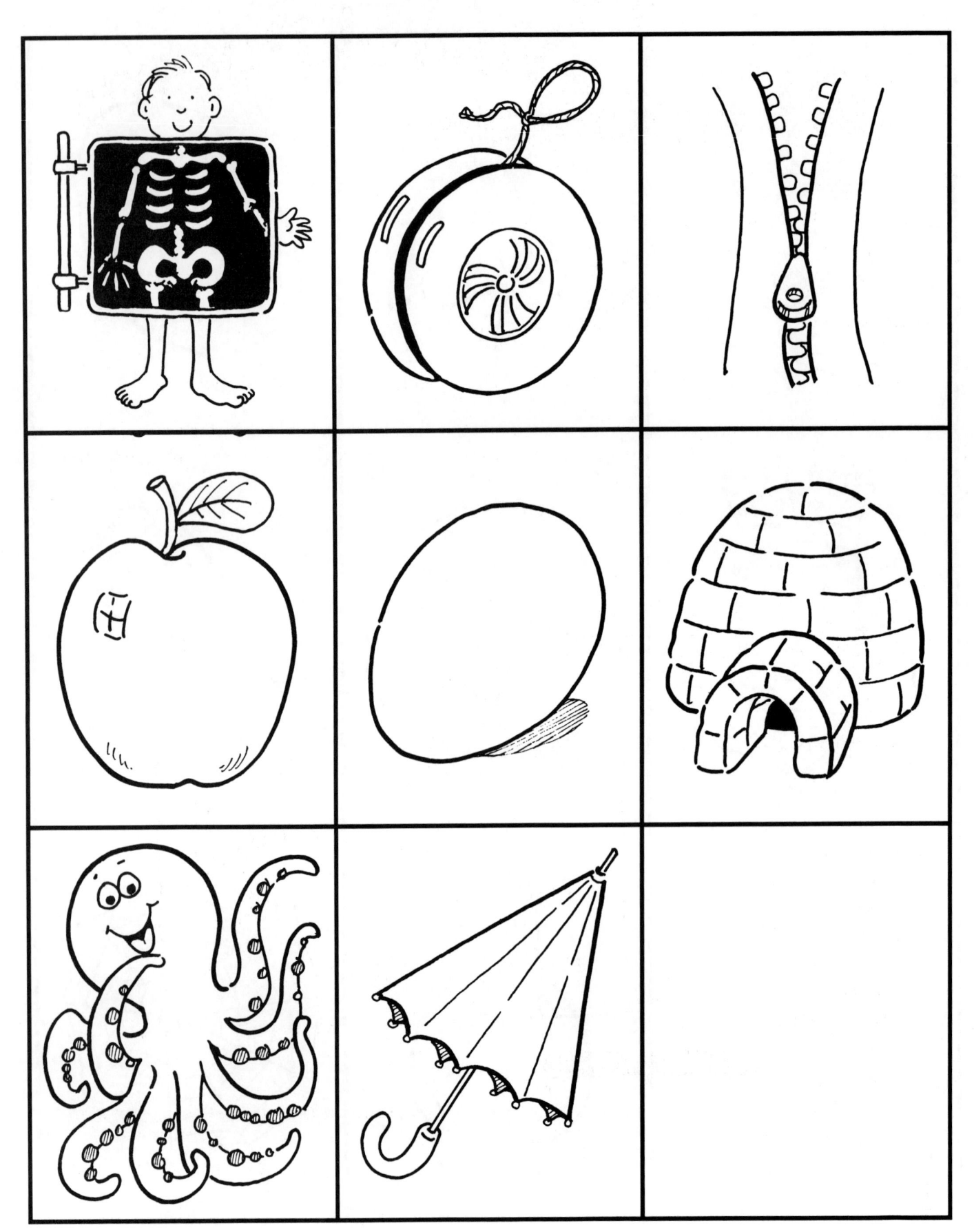

58 Decoding and Word Recognition

Acting out Vowel Poems

GET READY

- Vowel Poems (pages 60–61)
- chart paper
- crayons or markers
- highlighter

GET SET

Write each poem on a separate piece of chart paper. Draw a picture of some of the key words to give children visual clues. For example, for the Long *A* poem, draw a picture of a cake, a snake, and a lake. Highlight all the words with short or long vowels.

LANGUAGE CONCEPT

short and long vowels

GO!

1. Display the first poem. Divide the class into two groups.

2. Ask one group to pretend to be cats and dogs and act out the poem as the rest of the class reads it. Encourage the readers to emphasize the short *a* words.

3. Choose one of the short *a* words. Encourage the class to repeat the word and act it out (e.g., children say *cats* and act like cats).

4. Repeat the activity using a different poem.

Long A

Let's take a cake
To Jake the Snake.
Jake's having a party
By the lake.

VARIATION

- Encourage children to emphasize and act out the rhyming words in each poem.

Decoding and Word Recognition **59**

Short Vowel Poems

Short A
The cats took their naps
In my old hats.
Their naps were over
When the pups went "Yap!"

Short E
My pet Chet
Met your pet Jet.
They both met each other
At the vet.

Short I
Jim jumped in the waves
For a very chilly swim.
And all the little fish
Were swimming after him.

Short O
The frogs play leapfrog.
They don't want to stop.
But when it gets hot,
Into the pond they hop.

Short U
The slugs gave a rug
To their friends the bugs.
The bugs fell asleep
So nice and snug.

Decoding and Word Recognition

Long Vowel Poems

Long A
Let's take a cake
To Jake the Snake.
Jake's having a party
By the lake.

Long E
There's a beehive.
Don't you see?
Queen bee's chasing
You and me!

Long I
Mike and Ike
Like to bike.
Spike and Iris
Like to hike.

Long O
We wash my dog Rose
With the garden hose.
She shakes and shakes
From her toes to her nose!

Long U
We like to play
Our flutes in June
When frogs and crickets
Sing tunes to the moon.

Compound Word Partners

LANGUAGE CONCEPTS

compound words, reading sight words

GET READY

- Compound Word Cards (pages 63–64)
- red and blue paper

GO!

1. Give each child a word necklace. Have children take turns whispering their word in your ear.

2. Explain to children that they will find a partner to create a compound word. Give a few examples of compound words (e.g., headstand, eardrum, milkman).

3. Tell children that when they look for a partner, one person should have a red card and the other should have a blue card.

4. Invite children to sit down when they have found a partner.

5. Have partners say their compound word aloud to the class.

GET SET

Copy page 63 onto red paper and page 64 onto blue paper. Use the colored cards to make word necklaces (see page 4).

VARIATION

- For more of a challenge, copy all the cards onto white paper, and have children make compound words.

62 Decoding and Word Recognition

Compound Word Cards

flower	thumb
pig	sea
pop	hair
foot	bed
sail	lady

Compound Word Cards

pot	nail
pen	shell
corn	cut
ball	time
boat	bug

Let's Make a Word!

LANGUAGE CONCEPTS

letter sounds, blending sounds, digraphs

GET READY
- letter cards (pages 11–13)

GET SET
Copy and cut apart several sets of letter cards. Use them to make letter necklaces (see page 4). Each group of children will use a different set of letters, such as *s, t, o, p; t, a, p, e; p, i, n, k; c, a, p, e;* or *b, r, e, a, d.*

GO!

1. Divide the class into groups. The number of children in each group should be at least two more than the number of letter necklaces the group receives. For example, give the letter necklaces *s, t, o, p* to four different children, and ask the remaining children in the group to be "word-makers."

2. Have the word-makers arrange the children wearing letter necklaces to make words. Tell the word-makers they can use all or some of the letters to create words.

3. Have groups exchange letter necklaces with other groups. Designate new children as word-makers in each group, and encourage children to repeat the activity.

VARIATIONS

- Have children use digraph cards and letter cards to form words.
- Have children write down the words that they form. After groups have had a chance to use all sets of letter cards, meet as a whole group, and have children read some of the words they created.

Decoding and Word Recognition

Web-Go-Round

GET READY

- Digraph Word Cards (pages 67–68)
- construction paper
- scissors
- string or yarn
- stapler

SET

Write *th, sh, ch, fr*, and *bl* on large pieces of construction paper. Cut string or yarn into several 2' (61 cm) pieces. Place six pieces of string or yarn around the edges of each piece of paper to create a web (as shown). Staple the string or yarn to the paper. Make enough copies of the digraph word cards to give one to each child, and cut them apart.

LANGUAGE CONCEPT

digraphs

GO!

1. Give each child a word card. Direct children's attention to the webs, and tell them they need to find the web that corresponds with their word card. For example, if a child's card says *thank*, he or she would go to the *th* web. Have children sit next to one of the strings.

2. Have the children at each web stand up and read their word card one at a time to the rest of the class.

3. Have children trade cards, and repeat the activity.

4. Repeat the activity again. Then, staple the word cards to the string or yarn on the matching web. Hang the webs around the room for children to have as a reference for future use.

VARIATION

- Have children find the correct digraph web based on the ending of their word. For example, a child with the word *bush*, would sit at the *sh* web.

66 *Decoding and Word Recognition*

Digraph Word Cards

ship	shoe	she
shop	shut	frog
free	fry	from
chin	chair	chug

Digraph Word Cards

the	that	those
thank	thin	blue
block	blow	black
blame	chip	chat

Matt's Moving like a Monkey

LANGUAGE CONCEPTS

beginning letters and sounds, alliteration

GET READY
- name tags

GET SET
Make a name tag for each child.

GO!

1. Have children stand in a circle. Give each child a name tag and explain that they will be using the first letter of their first name for this game.

2. Call out a letter, and name an animal and a movement that begins with that sound (e.g., *If your name begins with M, go into the circle and move like a monkey*).

3. As children enter the circle, add their names to the alliterative sentence (e.g., *Matt and Mary are moving like monkeys*).

4. Repeat the activity using different letters. For example, for A say *act like an alligator*, for B say *bend like a bear*, and for C say *creep like a cat*.

> Matt and Mary are moving like monkeys.

VARIATIONS

- Change the refrain to *If your name begins with the sound /m/, go into the circle and move like a monkey.*
- Read aloud *The Z Was Zapped* by Chris Van Allsburg or *Some Smug Slug* by Pamela Duncan Edwards

Sight Word Wheel

LANGUAGE CONCEPT

reading high-frequency words

GET READY

- High-Frequency Word List (page 71)
- chalk
- index cards
- container
- music/cassette or CD player

GET SET

Use chalk to draw a wheel on the ground outside. Make enough spaces for each child to stand in one. Write one high-frequency word from the list in each space of the wheel. Write each word in the wheel on an index card, and place the cards in a container. Have music ready to play as the children walk around the wheel.

GO!

1. Invite children to stand on a word and say it aloud.
2. Begin the music, and encourage children to walk around the wheel.
3. Stop the music, and have children freeze on the nearest word.
4. Pick a card from the container, and display it. Have the class read it, and invite the child who is standing on that word to jump in the air.
5. Repeat the activity.

VARIATION

- Instead of playing music, children can chant the following verse as they walk around the wheel:
  Walking on the wheel,
  'Round and 'round I go.
  Which word I'll land on,
  Nobody knows.

70   Decoding and Word Recognition

High-Frequency Word List

a	does	like	over	too
about	down	little	part	two
after	each	long	people	up
again	even	look	place	use
all	find	made	put	used
also	first	make	right	very
an	for	man	said	was
and	from	many	same	water
another	get	may	see	way
any	go	me	she	we
are	good	more	so	well
around	had	most	some	went
as	has	much	such	were
at	have	must	take	what
away	he	my	than	when
back	help	new	that	where
be	her	no	the	which
because	here	not	their	who
been	him	now	them	why
before	his	number	then	will
but	how	of	there	with
by	I	off	these	word
called	if	old	they	words
came	in	on	things	work
can	into	one	think	would
come	is	only	this	write
could	it	or	three	years
did	its	other	through	yes
different	just	our	time	you
do	know	out	to	your

Word Taxis

GET READY

- Taxi Word Cards (page 73)
- letter cards (pages 11–13)
- yellow paper

GET SET

Copy the word cards on yellow paper, and use them to make word necklaces (see page 4). Make several copies of the letter cards, and use them to make letter necklaces for the letters in the word cards. For example, make letter necklaces *s*, *i*, and *p* for the word card *sip*. Designate areas in the room as "street corners."

LANGUAGE CONCEPTS

blending sounds, segmenting words, directionality

GO!

1. If you have 20 children, choose five of them to be the "taxi drivers," and give each driver a word necklace. Give the other children letter necklaces. (If you have 21–23 children, have five drivers and 15 passengers, and let the extra children direct traffic. If you have 24 children, have six drivers and 18 passengers, and so on.)

2. Assign children to stand at each "street corner." Make sure there are children with different letters at each corner.

3. Have the taxi drivers "drive" around the room. Encourage children to hail a taxi by saying *Taxi, taxi* and waving their hands if their letter is on the taxi driver's word necklace.

4. Ask the taxi drivers to stop at the street corners and pick up passengers. Have children board the taxi by forming a line behind the driver and placing their hands on the shoulders of the person in front of them. Note that if a child has *b* and there is already a *b* on the taxi, then he or she will have to wait for a different taxi.

5. Encourage children to arrange themselves in the correct order (from left to right) to form the "taxi word."

6. Have the passengers on each taxi say their individual letter sounds, and then encourage all the passengers to blend the sounds together to form a word (e.g., /h/, /o/, /p/, hop).

VARIATIONS

- Have older children form longer words.
- Have younger children form a "consonant taxi" and a "vowel taxi."

72 *Decoding and Word Recognition*

Taxi Word Cards

cot	fan
sip	jug
lot	den
bus	hop

Word Toss

GET READY

- High-Frequency Word List (page 71)
- poster board
- beanbags

LANGUAGE CONCEPT

reading sight words

GO!

1. Divide the class into groups of five to six children. Give each group a game board and a beanbag.
2. Have each group place the game board on the floor and stand in a line facing it.
3. Invite one child to toss the beanbag onto the game board and read the word that it lands on.
4. Have children take turns tossing the beanbag and reading the words.
5. Have groups trade game boards, and repeat the activity.

GET SET

Make a game board by drawing a 3 x 3 grid on poster board. Choose nine words from the word list, and write one word in each box of the grid. Make four to five grids, writing different words on each.

VARIATIONS

- For younger children, write a letter in each box of the game board.
- For older children, write a simple sentence in each box of the game board.

Decoding and Word Recognition

Magic "E" Relay

GET READY

- E Cards (page 76)
- Word Cards (page 77)
- scissors

GET SET

Make a copy of the E cards and the word cards, and cut them apart. Place the E cards on a table or the floor.

LANGUAGE CONCEPTS

final e, word formation, directionality

GO!

1. Divide the class into two teams, and have children pair off within a team. Give each pair a word card.

2. Have children line up in two single-file lines, about 10' (3 m) away from the E cards, for a noncompetitive relay race.

3. Have the first pair from each team run to the E cards. Encourage pairs to carry their word card together. Have pairs pick up an E card, add it to the end of their word, and sound out the new word.

4. As the pairs run back with their two cards, have them show their team the new word and pronounce the old word and the new one.

5. Ask those pairs to go to the end of their line, and invite the next pairs to continue the activity. Continue until every pair has had a turn.

6. Discuss with children how the vowel sound becomes a long vowel sound when the silent *e* is added.

VARIATION

- Have children form words using suffix cards (e.g., *-ed* or *-ing*) instead of E cards. Introduce the rule of doubling the last consonant before adding the suffix (e.g., *hop + p + ing*).

Decoding and Word Recognition

E Cards

e	e	e
e	e	e
e	e	e
e	e	e
e	e	e
e	e	e

Word Cards

cap	at
can	hid
kit	pin
cod	hop
not	cub
cut	tub

Vocabulary and Concept Development

ASSESSMENT & OBSERVATION QUESTIONS

- Can children identify and sort common words into basic categories?

- Can children describe common objects?

- Can children identify words and their opposites?

- Do children understand positional words?

Vocabulary and concept development refers to the children's understanding of the definition of words and the variety of contexts in which the words are used. In this section, children will have opportunities to practice identifying and sorting number, shape, and color words. They will also participate in activities that introduce them to action, position, and opposite words.

Musical Word Chairs

LANGUAGE CONCEPTS

reading color, number, and shape words

GET READY

- color, number, and shape word cards (pages 80–82)
- scissors
- tape
- bag
- music/cassette or CD player

GET SET

Copy and cut apart each set of word cards. Tape each card to a chair, and arrange the chairs in a large circle (as shown). Copy a second set of the word cards, cut them apart, and place them in a bag.

GO!

1. Have each child sit on a chair. Encourage children to read the word that is on their chair back.

2. Play music, and invite children to walk around the chairs. Stop the music, and have children sit down in the chair that is closest to them.

3. Pull a word card from the bag, and read it aloud. Encourage children to look at the word on their chair. Have the child with the word that you call find another chair that has the same type of word. For example, the child with the word *blue* finds another chair with a color word on it.

4. Have the two children exchange places, and repeat the activity.

VARIATIONS

- Have letters on the chairs rather than words.
- Have a rime on each chair. Call out an onset when the music stops, and have children blend it with the rime on their chair.
- Have class spelling or vocabulary words on the chairs.

Vocabulary and Concept Development

Color Word Cards

black	green	red
white	orange	blue
brown	purple	yellow

80 Vocabulary and Concept Development

Number Word Cards

one •	four ●●●●	seven ●●●●●●●
two ●●	five ●●●●●	eight ●●●●●●●●
three ●●●	six ●●●●●●	nine ●●●●●●●●●

Vocabulary and Concept Development **81**

Shape Word Cards

circle	rectangle	trapezoid
square	diamond	octagon
triangle	hexagon	pentagon

82 *Vocabulary and Concept Development*

People Word Wall

LANGUAGE CONCEPTS

reading and sorting color, number, and shape words

GET READY

- color, number, and shape word cards (pages 80–82)
- scissors
- sentence strips

SET

Copy and cut apart each set of word cards. Write *colors*, *numbers*, and *shapes* on separate sentence strips. Place the strips in a row on the floor. This area will be the "word wall."

GO!

1. Give each child one word card. Have children read their card.

2. Chant the following rhyme:
   *If you have a **color** word,*
   ***Gallop** to the word wall,*
   ***Gallop** to the word wall,*
   ***Gallop** to the word wall, one and all!*

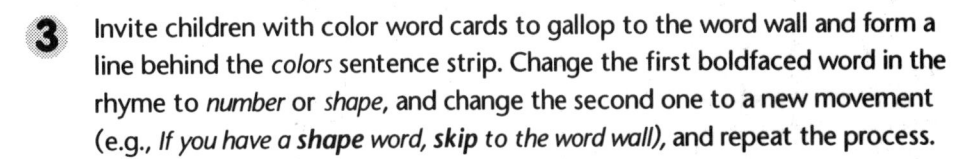

3. Invite children with color word cards to gallop to the word wall and form a line behind the *colors* sentence strip. Change the first boldfaced word in the rhyme to *number* or *shape*, and change the second one to a new movement (e.g., *If you have a **shape** word, **skip** to the word wall*), and repeat the process.

4. Have children trade word cards, and repeat the activity.

VARIATIONS

- Give more specific directions. For example, *If you have a color that is used to make purple, jump to the word wall* or *If you have a number less than five hop to the word wall.*
- Have children form a word wall according to the number of letters in their word or the beginning letter of their word.

Vocabulary and Concept Development **83**

Teacher, May I?

GET READY

- Action Word Cards (page 85)
- scissors
- chalk

GET SET

Make an enlarged copy of the action word cards to use as signs for children to read from a distance, and cut them apart. Use chalk to draw a starting line.

LANGUAGE CONCEPT

reading action words

GO!

1. Have children stand on the starting line and face you.

2. Hold the word cards, and position yourself about 20' (6 m) from the children. Show each card, and read aloud each word. Encourage children to read each word with you.

3. Pick one word card (e.g., *hop*), and display it for the class to read. Give an instruction to the entire class. For example, say *Hop three times*.

4. Tell children that they must say *Teacher, may I?* before they follow the direction. If a child forgets to say *Teacher, may I?*, send him or her back to the starting line.

5. Show different cards. Repeat the activity until all the children reach you.

VARIATION

- Give different movement instructions to individual children. For example, say *Johnny hop four times*. Johnny would reply *Teacher, may I?* before moving.

84 *Vocabulary and Concept Development*

Action Word Cards

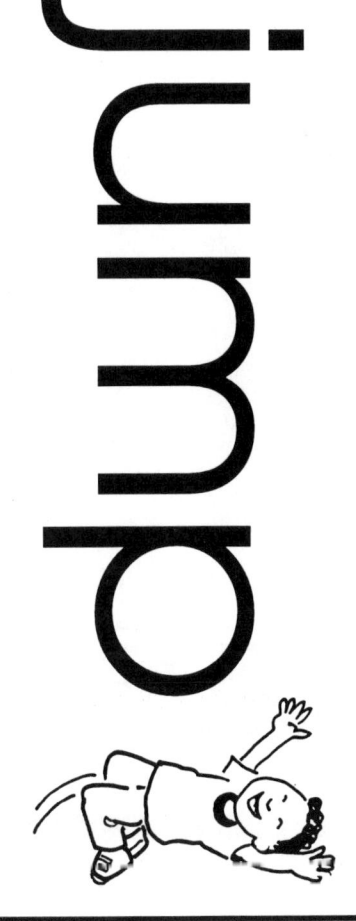

hop	skip
jump	tiptoe

Vocabulary and Concept Development **85**

Directional Poetry

GET READY

- Directional Poems (page 87)
- chart paper
- highlighter
- small rug or mat
- tape
- blue paper

GET SET

Write each poem on a separate piece of chart paper. Highlight the position words in each poem (e.g., *here, there, under*). For "Cat and Mouse Chase," lay a rug or mat on the floor, and tape a long, narrow piece of blue paper to the floor to be a stream. For "Dog and Cat Chase," use the same blue paper for a river.

LANGUAGE CONCEPT

reading position words

GO!

1. Display the poem "Cat and Mouse Chase."

2. Divide the class into two groups. Have one group act out the poem. Invite two children to make a "bridge" by joining hands and lifting their arms in the air. Have the rest of the children in the group act as cats and mice. Encourage the children in the other group to join you in reading the poem aloud and emphasizing the position words.

3. Display the poem "Dog and Cat Chase." Have the other group act out the poem as the rest of the class recites the poem aloud. Have two children make a "tunnel," one child act as a dog, four children be "trees" in the forest, and the rest of the group act as cats.

VARIATION

- Read aloud *Rosie's Walk* by Pat Hutchins (Simon & Schuster) or *Bears in the Night* by Stan and Jan Bernstain (Random House), and invite the class to act out the story.

86 *Vocabulary and Concept Development*

Directional Poems

Cat and Mouse Chase

The mice ran **here**.   (Point to a spot.)
The mice ran **there**.   (Point to another spot.)
The mice were running everywhere.

Under the bridge,
Over the stream,
Across the rug,
They ran as a team.

They ran to the **left**.   (Point to the left.)
They ran to the **right**.   (Point to the right.)
They ran from a kitty cat named Dwight.

Dog and Cat Chase

The cats ran **here**.   (Point to a spot.)
The cats ran **there**.   (Point to another spot.)
The cats were running everywhere.

Over the river
And **through** the wood,
They ran **through** the tunnel
As fast as they could.

They ran to the **right**.   (Point to the right.)
They ran to the **left**.   (Point to the left.)
They ran from a big brown dog named Jeff.

Vocabulary and Concept Development **87**

Opposites Attract

LANGUAGE CONCEPT

opposite words

GET READY

- Opposite Word Cards (pages 89–90)
- scissors

GET SET

Copy and cut apart the opposite word cards. Hide one card for each child around the room.

GO!

1. Invite children to move around the room to look for a word card. Tell children to each take just one card.

2. Encourage children to look for the person who has the card that is the opposite of their card.

3. Ask children to sit down once they have found their partner.

4. Invite partners to say their opposite words to the rest of the class.

VARIATIONS

- Give children half of one set of the opposite word cards, and hide the corresponding cards. Have children try to find the card that is the opposite of theirs.

- Make synonym cards, and encourage children to find the word card that means the same as their word.

88 *Vocabulary and Concept Development*

Opposite Word Cards

hot 	cold 
tall 	short 
happy 	sad 
clean 	dirty 
wet 	dry 

Vocabulary and Concept Development

Opposite Word Cards

hard 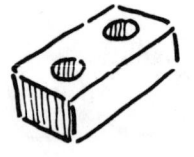	soft 
fast 	slow 
full 	empty 
night 	day 
near 	far 

Jungle Hike

GET READY

- scissors
- blue paper
- tape
- poster board
- beanbag
- hula hoops
- highlighter

GET SET

Position equipment and corresponding signs around the classroom or playground to create a "jungle hike." For example, cut a long, narrow piece of blue paper, and tape it to the ground. Write *Jump over the river* on a piece of poster board, and place the sign next to the blue paper. Use a beanbag for a rock and a hula hoop for a pond. Make a sign that reads *Throw a rock into the pond.*

LANGUAGE CONCEPT

reading position words

GO!

1. Read aloud each sign, and demonstrate how to go through the "jungle."

2. Review the position words, and encourage children to read them as they are going through the course.

3. Stagger the time each child starts the course so children go through the jungle one at a time.

VARIATION

- Invite children to create new obstacles and make new signs.

Vocabulary and Concept Development **91**

Charades

GET READY

- Charade Action Cards (page 93)
- scissors

LANGUAGE CONCEPT

describing action words

GO!

1. Invite one child to stand in front of the class, and have him or her pick one charade card.

2. Encourage that child to silently act out the word on the card.

3. Prompt the other children to guess what the word is.

4. Have the first child who correctly guesses the word repeat the process with a new card.

GET SET

Copy and cut apart the charade action cards.

VARIATION

- Have older children act out sentences or titles of books.

92 *Vocabulary and Concept Development*

Charade Action Cards

read	see	eat
run	crawl	fall
write	fly	laugh

Vocabulary and Concept Development 93

LANGUAGE SKILLS INVENTORY

	Recognizes and names uppercase letters	Recognizes and names lowercase letters	Writes uppercase letters	Writes lowercase letters	Follows words from left to right	Distinguishes a letter from a word	Recognizes that sentences are made up of words	Identifies rhyming words	Produces rhyming words	Distinguishes beginning sound	Distinguishes middle sound	Distinguishes ending sound	Blends phonemes to make a word	Changes or deletes a sound to change words	Counts syllables	Identifies consonant sounds	Identifies long vowel sounds	Identifies short vowel sounds	Forms compound words	Understands that as letters of words change so do the sounds	Reads high-frequency words	Sorts common words in basic categories	Describes common objects	Identifies opposite words

94 Language Skills Inventory

Language in Motion © 2000 Creative Teaching Press

Music & Literature Links

Music promotes movement and the use of gross motor skills. Use the suggested songs to teach language concepts and get the children moving. Read the recommended books to your class to reinforce language concepts such as alphabetical order, rhyming words, and alliteration.

SONGS
"ABC Rock" by Greg & Steve from *Kidding Around* (Youngheart Music)
"Apples and Bananas"
"Down by the Bay"
"The Name Game" and "Jump Rope Rhymes" by John Archambault and David Plummer from *Chicka Chicka Boom Boom and Other Coconutty Songs* (Youngheart Music)
"Rhyme Time 1 and 2" by Greg & Steve from *We All Live Together, Volume 1* (Youngheart Music)
"Willoughby Wallaby Woo"

ALPHABET BOOKS
A My Name is Alice by Jane Bayer (E. P. Dutton)
Chicka Chicka Boom Boom by John Archambault and Bill Martin Jr. (Aladdin)
Eating the Alphabet: Fruits and Vegetables from A to Z by Lois Ehlert (Harcourt Brace)
Old Black Fly by Jim Aylesworth (Econo-Clad)

RHYMING BOOKS
Each Peach Pear Plum by Janet and Allan Ahlberg (Penguin)
Hop on Pop by Dr. Seuss (Random House)
A House is a House For Me by Mary Ann Hoberman (Viking Press)
There's a Monster in the Tree by Rozanne Lanczak Williams (Creative Teaching Press)

ALLITERATION BOOKS
Alligators All Around: An Alphabet by Maurice Sendak (HarperCollins)
The Awful Aardvarks Go To School by Reeve Lindbergh (Viking Children's Books)
Some Smug Slug by Pamela Duncan Edwards (HarperCollins)
The Z Was Zapped by Chris Van Allsburg (Econo-Clad)

POETRY BOOKS
The 20th Century Children's Poetry Treasury by Jack Prelutsky (Knopf)
The Llama Who Had No Pajama: 100 Favorite Poems by Mary Ann Hoberman (Harcourt Brace)
Sing a Song of Popcorn: Every Child's Book of Poems by Beatrice Schenk de Regniers (Scholastic)
Where the Sidewalk Ends by Shel Silverstein (HarperCollins)

Gross Motor Skills Index

Activity	Page	Locomotor Skills	Nonlocomotor Skills	Balance Skills	Hand-Eye Coordination
A-Hunting We Will Go	6	X			
Alphabet Animal Exercises	14	X	X		
Alphabet Path	16	X			
Big and Little Letter Match	17	X			
Letter Circus	18		X		
Letter Magicians	19		X		
Sentence Scramble	20		X		
Name Hunt	24	X			
Slither like a Snake	25		X		
Walking It Out	26	X			
Bagging It Relay	28	X			
Cat, Cat, Bat	35	X			
Rime Buses	36	X		X	
Rhyme Hop-a-Long	38	X			
Rolling Rimes	40				X
Rime Tunnels	43	X			
Blending Endings Hopscotch	46	X		X	
Wiggle to the Sound	48	X	X		
Word Cheers	49	X	X		
You Put Your /H/ Hand In	50		X		
Jumping Jamboree	51	X			
Word Hunt	52	X			
Beginning Consonant Relay	55	X			
Acting out Vowel Poems	59	X	X		
Compound Word Partners	62	X			
Let's Make a Word!	65	X			
Web-Go-Round	66	X			
Matt's Moving like a Monkey	69	X	X		
Sight Word Wheel	70	X			
Word Taxis	72	X		X	
Word Toss	74				X
Magic "E" Relay	75	X			
Musical Word Chairs	79	X			
People Word Wall	83	X			
Teacher, May I?	84	X	X		
Directional Poetry	86	X	X		
Opposites Attract	88	X			
Jungle Hike	91	X	X		X
Charades	92	X	X		